better together*

*This book is best read together, grownup and kid.

 akidsco.com

a kids
book
about

a
kids
book
about

HOPE

by Kali Thorne Ladd

a
kids
book
about

Printed in the United States of America.

A Kids Book About books are available online: *akidsco.com*

To share your stories, ask questions, or inquire about bulk
purchases (schools, libraries, and nonprofits), please use
the following email address: *hello@akidsco.com*

Print ISBN: 978-1-958825-61-7
Ebook ISBN: 978-1-958825-62-4

Designed by Jelani Memory
Edited by Emma Wolf

This book is dedicated to the loves in my life, especially Brynn and Jordan, who breathe hope into existence.

This book is dedicated to the notion that even in darkness, there is light and that light can save us from our worst selves.

Intro

When I think about what drives one to do good in the world, to keep pushing despite adversity and setbacks, and to stay calm when it seems the world is falling apart—it is hope.

There is so much that our kids must navigate in today's world. Anxiety and depression are at all-time highs for our little ones. While this is clinical for some, for many others it is circumstantial or environmentally induced.

This book highlights how hope can be a critical antidote to navigating trying times. It underscores that hope exists within and outside of ourselves, and reminds us that it can always be found when we aren't able to feel it. Hope can inspire us individually and collectively to rise above current circumstances and create a future that is more beautiful and, well, hopeful.

This book does not suggest that hope is always the perfect solution, but as a life tool, it is perhaps one of the most powerful ones we can choose.

Did you know that right inside of you...

there is a power that is always present?

(Yes, I'm talking to you!)

Sometimes, it gets hidden deep down and can be hard to find.

But it's always inside you,
no matter what.

That power is called...

Hi. My name is Kali.

And I'm wicked* excited to talk
to you about hope today!

*When someone says this where I'm from, the East Coast,
it means they're **REALLY** excited to share something!

Hope is both a **noun** and a **verb**:

it's a thing and a way
of being in the world.

As a **noun**, hope is a feeling of trust that good things are possible, even when we're in a tough situation. Hope is believing that things can, and will, get better.

As a **verb**, hope is also an action.
When you are a hopeful person,
you become a catalyst*
for positive change.

*A catalyst is someone or something that makes change happen.

I come from a legacy* of hope...

*A person's legacy is all the things from
 the past that shape who they are today.

and I imagine you do too!
(Even if you don't know it).

My grandmother, Hattie Belle Jones,
lost both of her parents as a child.

Despite that grief and having
little money of her own,
she carried hope within her.

And this helped her keep moving
forward and give hope to her family,
community, and her place
of worship, a church.

My grandfather, Harold Thorne, was a first-generation American whose parents were from Barbados and Jamaica.

He worked 2, sometimes 3 jobs to support his family.

He hoped that his 3 sons could succeed, go to college, and achieve some of the successes he never could.

Sometimes hope is what you **say**.

And sometimes it's what you **do**.

My grandma had a way of making people feel like everything would be OK, no matter what.

My granddad helped people believe anything was possible, despite their circumstances—especially my dad.

Because my grandparents lived lives filled with and in pursuit of hope, my parents were born with this power all around them.

And that same hope has made me who I am today.

This is what hope **does**!

This is the **power** hope has.

It influences our actions and opportunities!

(And, you don't need grandparents like mine to have hope. It's true!)

Stories of hope are all around us.

Some come from family,
and others come from
people we don't even know.

Like people we read
about in books.

Or people we see on
television or in movies!

Hope is always near if we can just look
around us long enough to **notice**.

Where do you find hope around you?

Who brings you hope?

How do they help your hope grow?

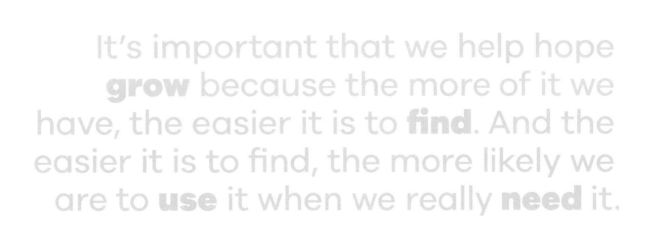

It's important that we help hope **grow** because the more of it we have, the easier it is to **find**. And the easier it is to find, the more likely we are to **use** it when we really **need** it.

While hope doesn't disappear, it can get covered up by sadness, fear, worry, or frustration.

Losing sight of hope is not an unusual thing; it's actually part of what it means to be **human**.

Knowing where hope lives, or may be hiding, is a really important thing.

Want to know something **cool**?

Both **people** *and* **things** have hope in them.

Things like
a beautiful
sunrise or
sunset,

a sky full
of stars,

or a towering
mountain.

Maybe hope is
in a vast ocean,

the petals
of a flower,

a stranger's
smile,

or the sound
of a friend's
laughter...

These wordless, beautiful things
can all bring hope.

And you may not be able
to explain why that is!

It's just something you feel.

In them, you're reminded
that everything will be...

THERE IS ALWAYS SOMETHI TO HOPE FOR!

NG

This is why being a hopeful person is important. We thrive when we feel and are surrounded by hope.

What does this look like?

Well, a hopeful person can:

offer a kind word,

remind someone how
important they are,

color a picture for a friend,

invite someone to
play who is alone,

help in their classroom,

or tell someone that what
they created is awesome!

Hope is like a window.

When windows are open, you can see, hear, and feel things you otherwise wouldn't experience.

When you live your life with hope,
you open a window of possibility.

This gives others the opportunity
to see, hear, and feel things
they otherwise wouldn't.

It brings a new perspective,
right when it is most needed.

How amazing is that?

When hope is hard to find,
call upon the hope within you
or around you to know that
things can and will get better.

Hope is a choice—a power
inside of you and a power
waiting outside of you.

Sometimes hope comes
very naturally, while other
times, it takes some work.

Its connection for each
person is different...

Hope is in reach for us all.

And so, I **hope** you remember this:

Neither your story, your circumstances, nor your identity dictate the hope you have or the hope you can gain.

Hope lives because you do.

Hope is your treasure to tend and hold in your heart.

May you always glimpse hope's glow and feel its warmth.

And, as you move through
this life, may you always
find ways to share hope.

Outro

Isn't hope AMAZING? As you finish reading this book, my wish is that you can see how pivotal hope is in navigating the terrain that is life. Hope inspires our kids when things are tough, but it can also inspire others, and even ourselves. I don't know about you, but my kids give me so much hope—they help me believe that better is possible.

In this way, hope is both one of the greatest gifts we can give our kids and a way for them to see the meaningful impact they have on us grownups.

Can you think of a time when hope carried you through difficulty or challenge?

What does hope look like, feel like, or sound like to you?

The more tangibly and realistically your kids can connect with and understand hope, the more they will be able to see how it shows up in their life. And hope will grow beyond an abstract concept to become a practical tool they can carry with them anywhere.

About The Author

Kali Thorne Ladd (she/her) wrote this book to empower any kid to understand the power of hope.

As "the only" Black kid in her community growing up, things weren't easy. Kali quickly discovered that hope was her light in the darkest times. It made the difference between pushing forward and giving up. Hope came from nature's beauty, family, faith, and a wild imagination.

Life can be tough. This book is meant to help kids see the power of hope to build resiliency. It is a resource to help those around us overcome tough things; if we can be a light to one another, it is game-changing and lifesaving.

 @kaliforchildren    @kali.ladd   @kalithorneladd

a
kids
book
about
BEING
INCLUSIVE

by Ashton Mota
& Rebekah Bruesehoff

a
kids
book
about
diversity

a
kids
book
about
LEADER-
SHIP

by Orion Jean

kids
boo
abo
IMMI

by MJ Calder

a
kids
book
about
SAFETY

by Soraya Sutherlin, CEM
partnership with JUDY

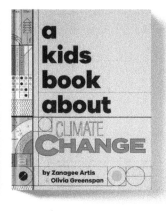
a
kids
book
about
CLIMATE
CHANGE

by Zanagee Artis
Olivia Greenspan

a
kids
book
about
IMAGINATION

by LEVAR BURTON

a
kids
book
about
CONFIDENCE

by Joy Cho

a
k
b

by

ls
ok
out
Pecia

Van

a
kids
book
about
NEURO-
DIVERSITY

by Laura Petix, MS OTR/L

a
kids
book
about
racism

by Jelani Memory

a
kids
book
about
RADICAL
DREAMING

by Alvin Schexnider

a
kid
boo
abo
bor

by KYLES

a
kids
book
about
VORCE

Ashley Simpo

a
kids
book
about
EQUALITY

by BILLIE JEAN KING

a
kids
book
about
CONSENT

by Karli Johnson

a
kids
book
about
PRIDE

by Kendall Clawson

a
k
b
a

by N

s
ok
ut
me

a
kids
book
about
BLENDED
FAMILIES

Discover more at akidsco.com

Printed in the USA
CPSIA information can be obtained
at www.ICGtesting.com
LVHW071525051123
762899LV00018B/63